Christma

Ten Poems to Surprise and Delight

ex libris

Candlestick Press

Published by:
Candlestick Press,
Diversity House, 72 Nottingham Road, Arnold, Nottingham UK NG5 6LF
www.candlestickpress.co.uk

Design and typesetting by Diversity Creative Marketing Solutions Ltd.,
www.diversity.agency

Printed by Ratcliff & Roper Print Group, Nottinghamshire, UK

Cover illustration © Katie Tooke, 2017

Candlestick Press monogram © Barbara Shaw, 2008

© Candlestick Press, 2017

ISBN 978 1 907598 54 8

Acknowledgements:

Thanks are due to all the copyright holders cited below for their kind
permission:

Simon Armitage, poem as yet unpublished, by kind permission of the
author.

Panya Banjoko, poem as yet unpublished, by kind permission of the author.

Alison Brackenbury, poem as yet unpublished, by kind permission of the
author.

Ian Duhig, poem as yet unpublished, by kind permission of the author.

Jonathan Edwards, poem as yet unpublished, by kind permission of the
author.

WN Herbert, poem as yet unpublished, by kind permission of the author.

Lorraine Mariner, poem as yet unpublished, by kind permission of the
author.

Pascale Petit, poem as yet unpublished, by kind permission of the author.

Gregory Woods, poem as yet unpublished, by kind permission of the
author.

Samantha Wynne-Rhydderch, poem as yet unpublished, by kind
permission of the author.

Contents

The Box

And if your father's lugging look he's lugging
something from the attic there he's tugging
Christmas from a box oh out it's coming
there! look from the cardboard, this fantastic

symbol or this tree that's evergreen
and plastic. Fix it up and deck it out
with toys and trinkets, stuff which does this – shines
or shimmers – if a present's placed beneath it

with no name-tag then bags I it's mine
or if it's yours then listen now I see it
it's smaller than these are. Hey the tree's a
diva: tinsel feather boas, baubles,

rock star's ear-rings, dangle look from all
its lugholes and what's next now but this tangle
of fairy lights, pimped-up barbed wire: plug
them in and mutter, mouth the magic words

so nobody can hear you swear and there!
they flash, they spark, they stir, sometimes they even
work and wrapping makes a mystery
of every present, rustles as they're opened,

whispering their secrets. If your father's
lugging look he's lugging from the attic
this box filled up with everything you were –
with tinsel, baubles, with this time last year.

Jonathan Edwards

Christmas Mother

When Maman arrived, robins
flew around the room
like blown kisses.

She brought in the green scent
of sunlight, her dress
rustled with ghost-leaves.

A brook was coiled on her head
in loops of auburn hair
with aquamarine banks

threaded with lizards and snakes,
and a mossy cascade
trickled down her nape.

Her hairpins were a shoal
of minnows that flitted
among her corkscrews,

and there were shallows
where crayfish hid
like porcelain clasps.

Crickets leapt from her chignon
onto the underwood of her temples
and her cheeks were terraces

where cicadas pulsed.
We heard the rain-crackle
of wrapping paper,

saw a storm released from its box
like a firecracker in the room
as she unfurled a map, revealed

her drawing of a vineyard
with two stone huts where we
could live together each summer.

I watched the kingfishers
of my mother's fingers
with their painted beaks

dive into pools of her hair,
while the cicadas
reached their noon crescendo

and stopped singing.
There was a colour around her face
I could not name,

but a garrigue
opened between us.
I crept over viaducts and cirques

trying to follow her into her gorge
where vultures soared,
their nests perched on the cliffs.

Then she left –

and I parted the mist
that rose like torn tissue
from her gift,
                        that rises still.

Pascale Petit

Santa circa 2092

On the Eve, when tongues of hung dead bells
lay silent, smog scraped the landscape
stretched its wrath across the shivering city.

Below a growling sky, the grey track of a sleigh
lugged by a pack of nine empty dogs
weaved between mounds of bones and rust.

Like a swarthy pioneer he handled the reins
hoping for a place to slap his sack, retrieve a song
from his memory, hang a sprig of mistletoe above a hearth.

Between carcasses of once lit haunts he dug
barehanded, searching for a glint of glitter, broken shells
of decorated baubles, a wayward ring of a bell.

He swept the musty ground, tore over hills,
followed a path of fallen fern, hooked his thumbs
into his belt, bellowed until the withered trees shook.

Night after night he roamed, scraped the days
from his boots, tugged at his bedraggled beard,
listened for life under the covering of dark.

With a sag for a smile and holes for eyes, he sat
whimpering amongst the ashen landscape, there
he set himself, back to a tree, slumped for the last.

As midnight struck, a wail clogged itself to the cracks
in his heart. Hidden in an undergrowth, threadbare
and feint, a woman, swollen, ready.

Panya Banjoko

Adoration of the Shepherds, a Night Piece

After Rembrandt's etching, The Hunterian, Glasgow

The description says Mary is "at rest" but really
what we have here is the total exhaustion
of someone who has just given birth
after riding on a donkey for five days.
She is swaddled like the baby. Is she looking at him
with love and wonder or has the inn-keeper
just woken her with his lamp?
If she does manage to turn her head
and see the men (and cow) peering in I doubt
she will acknowledge them. Joseph is reading.
A manual for first-time parents, the complete guide
to joinery? I suspect he will welcome this distraction.
Even my phone tells me that's enough now,
leave Mary be. The picture fades, goes black.

Lorraine Mariner

An Alien Christmas Carol

'there was no information, and so we continued'
TS Eliot

Imagine there's no Magi,
no Jesus and no crib -
just Eliot, Joseph Beuys,
and Lancelot Andrewes, sat
in your Modernist Advent calendar
in their sled drawn by camels Tatar.

Jupiter's in retrograde above
a bus shelter in Bethlehem:
this is how they keep Christmas real
for themselves, stand-ins who cannot feel
in their fingerless felt gloves
gifts of lard, thyme, and cumin.

A long train of slowing thought
has brought them to this caravanserai,
this spittal made unstable by
the cold blaze of descending light.
Because they cannot believe in luck
it has them, happed, rapt, in hope.

Because they cannot believe in accident
it taxes them, this UFO not fuelled
by faith, this Fiat von Daniken.
They are taken up by questions:
Is there a Rumi at the inn? When should they gather
at the shore of Lake Gallifrey?

Because they should be glad of another
lunch, the Galactic Mother
annointeth their heads
with the gravy of otherness,
serveth them the turkey of eternity,
the sprouts of salvation, and the holy roasts.

WN Herbert

White Rose Centre

Xmas again. My sole idea
was never again would I go to Ikea,
my sole hope that Mayans who, as I remember
had Doomsday arriving an earlier December,
meant this one so I had a prayer of sweet death,
salvation from which I could not hold my breath.
With time running out, I take the mall bus
blazed down one side *Shop Without Fuss!*
to White Rose's franchised Daedalian ark,
beside it, Ikea's a walk in the park.
Through aisles of mad shoppers where angels won't tread
I trudge like a zombie from 'Dawn of the Dead'
past fingernail bars and children's toy grottoes,
the walls full of posters with White Rose's mottoes:
Your Retail Soulmate! White Rose Says Yes!
I'd heard these before from the TV and press:
White Rose Loves Girls! White Rose Loves Boys!
White Xmas White Rose! More than white noise,
I notice they're choriambs, 'X' in Morse code.
They rat-a-tat-tat till I feel I'll explode
to its metre like that in an old Doctor Who
where this beat's the Master's mind-bending tattoo —
I write to it now, think in it still,
tapping my soul, sapping my will:
White Rose on Facebook @iamwhiterose
She changes faces more often than clothes:
Dorothy Perkins, Ann Summers, Monsoon,
Zara, Astarte, Hecate, the Moon.
The trochees and iambs are locked in their dance.
I listen and shuffle as if in a trance —
when suddenly, magically, it all makes sense:
before I'd been snobbish or selfish or dense.
Rose means much more than her minions can sell,
she offers redemption to poets as well,
the Rosa Candida of Dante from heaven
whose number is seven times seven times seven.

This makes my soul new, clap hands and sing,
I dance to her words: *What, This Old Thing?*
I Made You Look! She makes me see!
I love White Rose, my Belle Dame Sans Merci,
Empress of Free Verse, Queen of All Rhyme,
triple White Goddess for now and all time
for time to my Goddess means nothing at all —
like our new Doctor Who, it's at her beck and call.
I'll always love Rose in her every name,
whatever she looks like, I'll love her the same
in sickness as health, for richer or poorer,
not just Petrarch's muse, a poet this Laura,
my Rose of all Ridings from Yorkshire's to Graves':
like Santa she gives, like Jesus she saves;
I feel born again, more truly alive,
and if Doomsday dawns, White Rose will survive —
at first, the Four Horsemen may cast a cold eye
till they hear White Rose: then none shall pass by.

Ian Duhig

Mari Lwyd

Toys that spoke terrified my father. So did bells
and fairground horses skewered through gold poles

and the little song with which his aunt once trotted
him to bed: *up we go, one step two, taking the stairs*

like the ladies do. In Dorset Heart Clinic a nurse
read verses in his mother tongue thinking this

might help but when she lifted the twisted sheets
into pricked ears he wanted to bolt, afraid

of sharing his shroud with a talking horse.
This flicking of bedsheets took him back

to his boxroom in Gabalfa Street where every
New Year's Day the Mari Lwyd, the grey mare,

a horse's skull on a pole swathed in a white sheet
blinded by bottletop eyes would shake its mane

of red and blue ribbons at his window, demanding
entry in rhyming stanzas, its jaw worked by men

below while upstairs he'd be praying please please
that his father find the right rhymes to reply.

Samantha Wynne-Rhydderch

*The Mari Lwyd is the Welsh expression of a New Year custom known elsewhere
as 'mumming': with the aid of a horse's skull held aloft on a pole, a sheeted and
ribboned figure accompanies a spectral pony from door to door engaging in
poetic banter to gain entry.*

Bah... Humbug

Frost on the window-panes heightens the glamour of
                        flames in the ingle-nook.
Christmases future and past stand in line as if
                        Dickens's ghosts had to
queue for an omnibus, gloomily waiting to
                        utter their homilies
into the echo of legions of broadcasters'
                        lack of initiative.
Who but the dead could be warmed by their tedium?
                        This is a time for the
solace of solitude. Here's to the seasonal
                        renegades, sayers of
no to compulsory purchases, no to the
                        parlour games, no to all
kinds of togetherness. Here's to a Christmas of
                        mellow euphoria,
free from the pressures of workplace and family,
                        books to the left of you,
gin to the right, and a ghost of your own, singing
                        none of the songs that the
shops have been playing for weeks on a mind-numbing
                        loop. May your holiday
tender you (now that you've granted yourself that most
                        bracing of luxuries,
voluntary solitude) peace and tranquility!

Gregory Woods

A Twofold

Through snow like sleep that arrived
as we slept - the wall and the hedge
bandaged with snow -
snow felting the road

where we trod before light
leaving the door unlocked -
no goods to our name -
snow like a barn owl

or maybe a real owl actually swept
from the barn as we went so far
letting the child in us go
but keeping the smudged star

of the porch lamp in sight
to return through featherfall
bearing the lamb - bringing
the child in us home

through snow like sleep that arrived
as we slept - the wall and the hedge
bandaged with snow -
snow felting the road

where we trod before light
leaving the door unlocked -
no goods to our name -
snow like a barn owl

or maybe a real owl actually swept
from the barn as we went so far
letting the child in us go
but keeping the smudged star

of the porch lamp in sight
to return through featherfall
bearing the lamb - bringing
the child in us home.

Simon Armitage

My grandmother waits for Christmas

Amy Mary, labourer's child,
feared for food when harvests failed.
What did her mended stocking hold,
when thatched snow lit the house?
'An apple and an orange
and a sugar mouse'.

Factory's overtime revoked,
her children chose. Marge? Or jam?
Christmas hopes, at tea, provoked
Amy Mary's list. Her house
hummed along. My mother sang
'AND a sugar mouse!'

I met Christmas on the hop,
with Fairtrade chocolates; one lean year
a toy dog from the local shop.
In City suit, in our small house,
suddenly my daughter chants
'and a sugar mouse'…

Grey, with loot, I bounce the bus.
At dawn, in dream, before the trussed
presents, rain, descend on us,
I nibble, in that kind dark house,
on the crystal crust
of my sugar mouse.

Alison Brackenbury